DIRECTIONS IN DEVELOPMENT

Managing Commodity Booms—
and Busts

Panos Varangis, Takamasa Akiyama, and Donald Mitchell

The World Bank
Washington, D.C.

Library of Congress Cataloging-in-Publication Data

Varangis, Panayotis N.
    Managing commodity booms—and busts / Panos Varangis,
Takamasa Akiyama, Donald Mitchell.
        p.   cm. — (Directions in development)
    Includes bibliographical references (p. 21)
    ISBN 0-8213-3489-1
    1. Commodity futures—Developing countries. 2. Primary
commodities—Prices—Developing countries—Forecasting.
3. Export marketing—Government policy—Developing countries.
I. Akiyama, T. (Takamasa), 1944– . II. Mitchell, Donald, 1947– .
III. Title. IV. Series: Directions in development (Washington, D.C.)
HG6051.D44V37   1995
332.63'28—dc20   95-42336
                                                                                  CIP

The authors are grateful to all those who helped in producing this booklet,
particularly M. Ahmed, J. Cuddington, A. Kraay, S. Lateef, J. McIntire,
Y. Mundlak, J. Salop, A. Ray, and M. Schiff for their useful comments. The
authors bear sole responsibility for the views expressed. The editors were
Meta de Coquereaumont, Paul Holtz, Vince McCullough, and Bruce Ross-
Larson, all with American Writing Corporation.

Contents

Foreword

In developing countries dependent on a few commodities for their exports, booming commodity markets can be beneficial or detrimental depending how they manage the windfalls. Two key problems need to be addressed: the fluctuations in income, and transitory bonanzas in foreign exchange earnings. This second effect, in particular, is likely to cause the exchange rate to appreciate above its long-term sustainable level.

The lessons from experience are clear: countries that have managed to invest the gains from the boom come out of it stronger and with higher rates of growth. Countries that, through misguided policies, consume the windfall gains and allow production to shift from exports to domestic markets have nothing to show for it at the end of the boom and find it difficult to undo the misalignment in relative prices produced by the boom.

This booklet focuses on the management of commodity price volatility from the perspective of developing countries. It examines and contrasts government policies and institutional and marketing structures that have proven to be effective in managing commodity booms—and busts.

Michael Bruno
Senior Vice President, Development Economics
and Chief Economist

Summary

Booming commodity markets can bring economic good or ill to developing countries that are exporting these commodities, depending on how these countries handle the windfalls. Such booms occur roughly once every ten years. The latest began in 1992 and, while most commodity prices have probably peaked, developing countries still have an opportunity (albeit brief) to improve their fiscal positions while prices remain high.

The economies of developing countries are heavily dependent on commodities. Primary commodities, including energy, account for, on average, nearly one-half of export revenues from developing countries. Any boom in commodity prices means a boom in government revenues. In the past, policymakers have often mismanaged the boom. When prices fall, these economies are left in worse shape than before.

When revenues from commodity exports increase, governments are tempted to make long-term spending commitments based on what turn out to be short-term price rises. Witness Colombia, Kenya, and Tanzania after coffee prices boomed in the late 1970s. In the post–oil boom Nigeria of the 1970s and early 1980s, the shortfall of revenues was so severe that external borrowing had risen dramatically even before oil prices began to fall. It was much the same story in Venezuela's and Mexico's handling of their oil booms.

Recent research shows that fluctuating GDP and investments are detrimental to long-term economic growth. Hence fiscal policy should be countercyclical. Governments experiencing booms, however, tend to adopt a procyclical fiscal policy because of the windfall tax revenue.

Moreover, foreign exchange earnings almost always soar during times of higher commodity prices, which can lead to an excessive appreciation of the real exchange rate. This could make some tradable sectors less competitive in global markets and, ultimately, lead to a decline in domestic production in other, nonbooming sectors. This is sometimes known as Dutch disease, after the experience of the Netherlands in the 1960s following the discovery (and export boom) of North Sea gas.

Another problem associated with commodity booms is a slowdown in diversification. Since producers often have few investment alternatives, windfall revenues are invested in the booming commodity subsectors—

even when producers are aware that the boom is temporary. This can lead to overcapacity and much lower prices later and can have long-term effects on a country's diversification efforts. Liberalizing and developing financial markets can provide alternative investments. Underdeveloped domestic financial and capital markets, however, may not be much of a problem if producers can invest freely abroad.

Trade policies can also partly determine the effects of a commodity boom. If they prevent revenues from being spent on imports, trade restrictions may lead to further appreciation of the exchange rate.

Learning from experience

In the past, governments introduced various policies to manage booms and avoid the onset of Dutch disease. They have followed prudent fiscal policies, lifted import and capital restrictions, tightened monetary policies, accumulated foreign reserves, and reduced foreign debt. But what were the specific measures, and how effective were they?

Export taxes. In the latest coffee boom, Cameroon, Côte d'Ivoire, Honduras, Uganda, Viet Nam, and others reintroduced export taxes. Such taxes, so the argument goes, can alleviate both the spending and the resource movement effects of the boom and protect nonbooming tradable sectors. Tax revenues should be invested in high-yielding public investment programs that increase long-term growth. Maintaining high standards of project evaluation is also important.

In practice, however, tax rates are usually set too high and public investment projects are often selected on noneconomic grounds. This has damaged the booming sector with little compensation elsewhere in the economy. High export taxes also encourage tax evasion and smuggling.

Commodity boom bonds. These are bonds denominated in foreign currency held by local exporters of commodities. The bonds can be considered as forced savings in foreign currency. Their purpose is to protect the economy of the commodity-exporting country from the effects of a sudden inflow of foreign exchange. For example, due to a rise in commodity prices in Colombia the central bank issued "coffee bonds" to Colombian coffee producers in exchange for foreign currency earned from exports. Coffee exporters were required to hold a certain percentage of their dollar-denominated revenues in these bonds.

Hedging instruments. Governments and the private sector can make future revenues more predictable by using options, futures, and swaps. The Mexican government used such hedging tools to ensure a guaranteed price for its oil (and predictable revenues) after the Gulf war. Traders and producers, too, could benefit from hedging. Some developing countries would have trouble in using hedging instruments, however. Also, hedging can be costly, requires good credit ratings, and is more effective when used to cover commodity prices for a relatively short period of time—about a year for most commodities.

Revenue stabilization funds. Another way to manage commodity price shocks is to create a stabilization fund to stabilize government expenditures (not to support or stabilize commodity prices). By saving resources in boom years, governments can reduce the need to cut spending in leaner times. A well-designed fund can smooth expenditure adjustments upward and downward. However, funds often run into difficulties because of the unpredictable nature of commodity prices or mismanagement of fund resources.

International commodity agreements. During the late 1970s and the 1980s many commodity-producing countries attempted to stabilize commodity prices (coffee, cocoa, and rubber, for instance) through international agreements. Only the rubber agreement is still in force—though barely—and its effectiveness is being questioned by some signatories.

How to manage a boom

Commodity prices are especially hard to predict. Crops (and so prices) can be affected by weather, insects, and disease. And world prices can be influenced by speculators and political events in exporting and importing countries. Such uncertainties make any kind of planning difficult. Even so, experience has shown that countries that adopted prudent fiscal and monetary policies, accumulated reserves, reduced foreign debt, and liberalized capital controls and import restrictions saw long-term beneficial results from commodity booms. Other, complementary policies have also been suggested. These policies could provide additional benefits, depending on the conditions of the economies concerned and the nature of the boom. Policies employed to manage commodity windfall revenues are:

Don't overspend or overcommit. Governments should not commit to long-term spending levels that they cannot sustain when the boom fizzles.

Adopt prudent monetary and fiscal policies. Commodity-dependent economies are more vulnerable to external shocks, making good macroeconomic policies especially critical. Countries should follow prudent monetary and fiscal policies, and they could even consider reducing external debt with the proceeds from the boom. In many cases a rigid budgetary process during a boom can result in inefficient use of the windfall revenue (as when the revenue accrues to one ministry). Governments should consider modifying the budgetary process during booms. Also, governments experiencing commodity booms tend to spend the windfall tax revenue from the boom. This procyclical fiscal policy approach makes a country's GDP fluctuate more—and thus should be avoided.

Reduce controls. Capital-account controls (restrictions on investing abroad) and import controls should be reduced. Policymakers shou d consider taking advantage of the favorable trade balance situation to ase import restrictions. This will help avoid a real exchange rate apprecia ion and will improve economic efficiency. Then, when the boom ends, the economy will be in better condition than it was before the boom.

Diversify and adjust. It is less painful to begin such programs when prices are high, and booming sectors will be better able to cope with lower commodity prices when the boom subsides.

A revenue stabilization fund may be an option under some circumstances. It can smooth adjustments in spending when the boom is over. Funds can be useful when domestic financial markets are not well developed and there are significant adjustment costs to booms and busts. However, funds often encounter financial difficulties and are subject to mismanagement.

Hedge. The use of market-based hedging instruments (futures, options, swaps) makes commodity-related revenues more predictable, increases the probability that anticipated revenues will be realized, and improves the ability of policymakers to plan. Hedging instruments can be used independently or to complement a stabilization fund in order to iron out flows into and from the fund.

Avoid heavy export taxes. They may encourage tax evasion and smuggling. Moreover, governments tend to spend incremental tax revenues swiftly and poorly. Low to moderate export taxes (acting as a windfall profit tax), however, could have beneficial effects in reducing overinvestment in the booming sector and providing incentives for diversification.

Because the track record of governments in managing booms and busts is far from impressive, the private sector should be allowed to manage a larger share of windfall profits. However, the management of windfall profits by producers may still be frustrated by distortions such as capital account controls, trade restrictions, and macroeconomic instability. To facilitate private management, governments should remove these distortions by pursuing trade and financial liberalization.

Why booms happen

Booming commodity prices can help or hurt developing-country economies that export these commodities, depending on how governments handle (or mishandle) the boom and, more particularly, how they spend the windfall export revenues.

Although most commodity price fluctuations are subject to long-run cycles, there are also short-term variations (booms or busts) whose effects are in essence quite similar. Commodity booms happen every ten years or so. The longest and strongest booms were the two in the 1970s, when prices rose by 240 percent in nominal terms; the most recent boom began in 1992. And although there are some similarities between the 1970s and the latest price increases, there are also some important differences (box 1).

The recent surge in prices appears to be based on supply shocks, not on increased demand. This suggests that prices will fall as production returns to normal or higher levels. Although many commodity prices have probably peaked, developing countries still have an opportunity (albeit brief) to improve their fiscal positions before prices fall.

Most exports of developing countries are in primary commodities. Including energy, these accounted for 76 percent of Africa's merchandise exports in 1992 and 47 percent of merchandise exports for all low- and middle-income countries. For severely indebted countries, the figure was 61 percent. Fuels, minerals, and metals make up about 29 percent of developing-country export earnings, with agricultural products (including timber) accounting for another 18 percent.

Thus developing countries rely on commodities for much of their export earnings. The latest boom has favored these countries because the prices of the commodities they export (such as coffee, cotton, and copper) have generally risen more than the prices of those that they import (grains, petroleum, and so on). Higher cotton prices benefited countries in Sub-Saharan Africa and Central Asia; Latin American export revenues rose on the back of booming copper prices and higher coffee prices, which also benefited Sub-Saharan Africa.

Uncertainties associated with commodity booms make any kind of planning difficult. Bumper years are often followed by busts that typically leave real prices lower than before. When revenues from commodity exports increase, governments are tempted to make long-term spending commitments based on what turn out to be short-term price rises (as happened in the 1970s). Moreover, the increases in foreign exchange earnings often associated with higher commodity prices can lead to excessive—and prolonged—appreciation of the real exchange rate. This could make some tradable sectors less competitive and, ultimately, lead to a decline in domestic production in other sectors, notably manufacturing. Commodity booms also hold back diversification into other export commodities.

Box 1. Boom, boom

The recent commodity boom differs from that of the 1970s in several ways. In 1973 the prices of two of the most sensitive commodity groups (grains and energy) increased sharply. Although grain prices have risen this year as well, their 25 percent rise is far below the doubling of prices that took place in the 1970s. This might be why the current boom has not attracted much attention. Moreover, the Soviet Union, which imported large quantities of grain in the early 1970s, no longer exists, and the import demand of the newly independent states is severely curtailed by foreign exchange constraints and weak economies.

Fertilizer prices have risen recently because of production capacity constraints and sharp increases in demand, but by less than in the 1970s. This means that the crop yield effects of higher fertilizer prices are less today than during the 1970s. In the unlikely event that petroleum prices move sharply upward, the increase in fertilizer prices should be reversed as production responds to higher prices.

Another difference between the two booms is the role of commodity funds. The emergence of large commodity funds in the 1980s has perhaps caused some changes in commodity market fundamentals. The emergence of funds has increased competition among those willing to hold commodity stocks and has increased the arbitrage possibilities in the market (prices respond faster to events). At times, funds may have accentuated commodity price trends. Some analysts have found an association between fund activities and the level of prices during 1994 for certain commodities, such as cocoa and metals.

Although the price rises for some commodities have been large, they scarcely compensate for the declines of the past decades. Aluminum prices, for instance, have yet to approach the highs of the mid-1980s. Coffee, which has more than doubled in price in the past year, is still at less than 30 percent of the peaks reached in the 1970s. Cotton, cocoa, and copper prices are about one-third of the highs of the 1960s and 1970s in real terms. And while petroleum prices have increased recently, they are still below their 1992 and 1993 levels.

Why this boom won't continue

A commodity boom is a sharp price rise in a number of commodities over a relatively short period of time (of up to about two to three years). The increases since late 1992 have certainly been sharp and broadly based. The World Bank's index of 33 nonfuel primary commodity prices rose 42 percent, from a low in October 1992 to a high in March 1995 (figure 1 and table 1). Food prices increased 21 percent, and the index of agricultural raw materials was 54 percent higher. Metal and mineral prices did not increase significantly until late 1993, when they bounced upward, increasing 41 percent through January 1995.

Figure 1. Weighted index of primary commodity prices for low- and middle-income economies

Petroleum (spot)

Index: current US dollars (1990=100)

Nonfuel commodities

Index: current US dollars (1990=100)

Total food

Index: current US dollars (1990=100)

Metals and minerals

Index: current US dollars (1990=100)

Note: Total food and metals and minerals are included in the nonfuel commodities index. Food is weighted by 29.4 in the nonfuel commodities index and metals and minerals by 28.1.
Source: Commodity Policy and Analysis Unit, International Economics Department, World Bank.

Why the recent surge in prices? Declining commodity prices through-out the 1980s led to reduced investment in production capacity, which

Table 1. Weighted index of primary commodity prices for low- and middle-income economies in current dollars

1990=100

	Petroleum (100.0)	Nonfuel commodities Total	Agriculture Total (69.1)	Food Total (29.4)	Grains (6.9)	Fats and oils (10.1)	Other (12.4)	Beverages (16.9)	Raw materials Total (22.8)	Timber (9.3)	Metals and minerals (28.1)	Fertilizers (2.7)
Annual												
1980	161.1	126.3	136.9	139.2	134.3	148.6	134.3	185.1	104.3	79.0	95.1	128.9
1981	155.1	108.6	116.3	122.9	143.3	141.7	96.0	148.8	89.9	88.4	83.3	122.3
1982	142.7	95.9	104.0	96.6	105.7	117.4	74.5	149.5	79.9	66.1	75.2	104.9
1983	129.6	103.3	112.3	105.4	109.6	135.6	78.2	157.2	87.9	63.7	81.9	96.1
1984	124.6	105.1	118.0	106.9	104.3	157.7	66.7	179.6	67.0	68.9	74.1	97.7
1985	118.8	91.7	100.5	86.3	89.2	113.0	62.9	165.3	70.8	50.1	70.2	89.0
1986	62.7	92.6	103.8	77.1	76.6	87.7	68.6	195.7	70.5	63.9	65.4	69.3
1987	79.3	92.9	98.8	84.5	77.5	101.2	74.7	135.6	80.2	80.3	76.4	94.4
1988	64.3	111.3	110.1	107.3	102.2	133.7	88.5	141.2	90.6	80.4	114.6	108.7
1989	78.0	107.5	108.0	107.9	112.0	119.1	96.5	115.0	96.9	93.2	111.3	106.2
1990	100.0	100.0	100.0	100.0	100.0	100.0	100.0	100.0	100.0	100.0	100.0	100.0
1991	84.7	95.5	97.9	99.2	101.7	104.5	93.3	93.6	99.1	104.2	86.9	102.4
1992	83.1	92.1	94.4	100.0	101.7	111.7	89.5	79.4	98.3	114.5	86.1	95.8
1993	73.6	91.6	99.1	98.6	93.6	111.5	90.7	84.9	110.3	152.4	74.0	83.7
1994	69.4	111.9	123.7	106.8	102.1	126.0	93.8	150.4	125.8	156.6	84.6	93.4
Quarterly												
2Q94	70.7	105.4	116.5	102.8	96.6	122.7	89.9	126.2	127.0	163.4	79.3	93.1
3Q94	74.4	122.2	137.9	105.8	95.4	126.1	95.1	201.5	132.2	165.9	86.6	93.6
4Q94	72.1	122.5	133.3	110.8	101.9	135.9	95.3	177.8	129.5	149.3	98.5	96.3
1Q95	75.1	126.3	136.4	113.4	104.9	135.1	100.4	169.2	141.9	142.1	103.6	101.7
2Q95	79.3	124.2	134.9	112.6	110.5	131.0	98.8	163.7	142.2	143.1	100.2	102.6
3Q95	71.9	120.5	128.0	119.5	128.4	136.1	100.9	145.7	125.9	138.5	103.7	102.6
Monthly												
1994 Jan	61.8	95.8	105.8	109.2	121.8	122.7	91.0	92.5	111.1	147.9	71.9	89.9
1994 Feb	60.2	98.1	107.8	109.3	117.8	116.2	97.5	95.7	114.8	146.1	74.9	90.2
1994 Mar	59.5	98.6	106.3	105.4	103.8	117.0	96.9	100.6	117.8	148.8	75.4	91.1
1994 Apr	65.9	99.5	109.9	103.7	101.8	118.0	93.1	102.9	123.2	157.8	74.6	92.3
1994 May	71.2	105.9	117.2	102.7	95.3	123.3	90.0	128.6	127.3	164.2	79.5	93.6
1994 Jun	75.0	110.7	122.4	101.8	92.7	126.8	86.6	147.1	130.5	168.4	83.9	93.6
1994 Jul	78.1	121.9	137.5	102.6	90.4	120.6	94.6	203.3	133.7	167.3	86.5	93.6
1994 Aug	74.3	120.2	135.7	105.8	95.9	126.8	94.1	192.2	132.5	167.7	84.7	93.6
1994 Sep	70.8	124.6	140.5	109.2	99.9	130.8	96.7	209.0	130.2	162.7	88.7	93.6
1994 Oct	72.0	121.9	135.1	106.9	101.8	128.5	92.0	192.9	128.7	152.9	92.2	95.5
1994 Nov	74.7	122.5	132.6	110.5	101.2	138.8	92.5	177.5	127.9	149.9	100.3	96.7
1994 Dec	69.7	123.1	132.3	115.2	102.8	140.4	101.4	163.0	131.8	145.2	102.9	96.7
1995 Jan	73.6	126.1	134.3	111.7	104.6	134.7	96.9	166.5	139.7	147.8	108.5	100.1
1995 Feb	75.8	126.0	136.6	115.1	104.7	135.2	104.5	166.6	142.1	141.4	102.2	102.6
1995 Mar	75.8	126.6	138.4	113.4	105.5	135.4	99.8	174.4	143.9	137.2	100.1	102.6
1995 Apr	81.5	126.3	137.5	111.2	104.4	131.0	98.7	170.5	147.2	141.4	101.0	102.6
1995 May	80.5	124.6	136.4	111.5	108.8	129.6	98.2	167.1	145.7	143.8	97.7	102.6
1995 Jun	75.9	121.9	130.8	115.2	118.2	132.6	99.3	153.5	134.0	144.5	101.9	102.6
1995 Jul	75.9	121.6	129.2	121.7	127.8	138.5	104.5	145.0	127.0	141.8	105.0	102.6
1995 Aug	72.0	121.3	128.6	118.2	125.4	134.2	101.0	152.9	124.1	138.5	105.1	102.6
1995 Sep	73.5	118.3	126.1	118.6	131.8	135.6	97.2	139.2	126.1	135.3	100.6	102.6

Note: Weighted by average 1987–89 export values for low- and middle-income economies.
Source: Commodity Policy and Analysis Unit, International Economics Department, World Bank.

led to supply deficits in the early 1990s. This was followed by poor harvests, and beginning in late 1992 prices began to climb. Despite the recent downturn, prices could move higher in the short run. The longer-term picture, however, is less than rosy.

The World Bank's index of primary commodity prices is expected to increase by 8.6 percent in nominal terms in 1995 and then decline in 1996 and 1997. In real terms, it is projected to decline 8 percent by 2000 from the March 1995 peak and remain near that level for the next five years. Cotton prices are expected to rise another 19 percent in 1995; this follows an increase of 38 percent in 1994. Grain prices are expected to rise in 1995, with maize, rice, and wheat all higher.

Agricultural commodities. The boom in agricultural prices began with rice and an unusually poor harvest in Japan in the summer of 1993. Japanese rice imports rose from zero in 1992 to 2.2 million tons in 1993. World prices almost doubled but fell just as sharply when Japan's production recovered in 1994. Also in the summer of 1993, the United States maize crop was slashed by a third because of flooding in the Midwest. Maize prices soared but lost all that ground by November 1994 as US production recovered.

It was the same story of poor harvests for other commodities. Insect damage reduced the world's cotton crop, while Cuba's sugar production continued to decline. Four major cotton producers—China, India, Pakistan, and the United States—reported much lower crops in 1993. World production has recovered substantially since, but disease and pest problems in China and South Asia are delaying a full global recovery.

In 1994 supply disruptions also extended to coffee. Brazil lost an estimated 40 percent of its crop because of frost and drought. At the same time, world coffee stocks were at their lowest level since 1979. Prices soared. Cocoa prices, which had fallen by 70 percent in real terms from 1984 to 1992, have increased, too—by 60 percent from mid-1993. Cocoa price increases were not due to weather disruptions but to adjustments in demand and supply following a period of very low prices. Still, cocoa prices are very low by historical standards.

Metals and minerals. An increase in global demand and a reduction in world stocks have pushed metal and mineral prices higher. Voluntary production cutbacks and restructuring in mining, processing, and fabrication have also tightened supplies and increased prices further for some metals. Higher metal prices have been partly credited to speculative buying by commodity funds. If so, the boom in prices will be short-lived and may already be over for many metals.

Crude oil. After shortages during the Gulf war, oil supplies picked up in 1993 and prices fell significantly, before rebounding in the second quarter of 1994. World oil demand will probably grow modestly for the rest of the 1990s, and crude oil prices are unlikely to rise much, especially if Iraqi crude reenters world markets.

The revenue windfall

For many developing countries, primary commodities still account for the lion's share of export revenues. In 1993–94 the average price of primary commodity exports rose 19 percent. The effects on the revenues of individual countries was often much greater because of the concentration in a few booming commodities. Complete export revenue figures are not yet available, but the World Bank has estimated revenues for eight agricultural commodities—cocoa, coconut oil, coffee, cotton, groundnut oil, palm oil, rubber, and soybean oil—and three metals—aluminum, copper, and nickel—for all low- and middle-income countries (table 2). Agricultural exports accounted for 70 percent of the total increase in export revenues, and coffee for half the increase in agriculture exports.

The gains from higher export prices were widespread (table 3). Latin America and the Caribbean notched up the largest gains, followed by East Asia and the Pacific. Latin America and the Caribbean benefited most from the boom in coffee prices, although other commodities, including metals, also contributed. For East Asia and the Pacific, the increase was due mostly to higher prices for rubber, coffee, palm oil, and other vegetable oils.

Which countries were the big winners? In dollars, Malaysia registered the biggest gain ($1.76 billion). Palm oil led the way ($1.36 billion), followed by rubber ($340 million). The other leaders were mainly coffee exporters. Brazil benefited the most, despite its coffee production

Table 2. Export revenues from major primary commodities for low- and middle-income countries
(billions of dollars)

Commodity	1992	1993	1994	Increase, 1993–94
Agricultural commodities	18.0	18.5	28.2	9.7
Cocoa	2.2	2.2	2.7	0.5
Coconut oil	0.8	0.5	0.7	0.2
Coffee	5.2	5.8	10.6	4.9
Cotton	2.6	2.4	2.8	0.5
Groundnut oil	0.1	0.2	0.2	0.1
Palm oil	2.8	3.1	4.9	1.8
Rubber	3.5	3.3	4.6	1.3
Soybean oil	0.9	1.1	1.5	0.5
Metals and minerals	14.4	13.8	17.8	4.0
Aluminum	4.9	5.2	7.2	2.0
Copper	8.1	7.2	8.7	1.4
Nickel	1.4	1.4	1.9	0.6

Source: Estimates by the Commodity Policy and Analysis Unit, International Economics Department, World Bank.

problems. Colombia, too. Indonesia was also high up among the winners, with large gains in export revenues from rubber ($400 million),
palm oil ($300 million), and coffee ($300 million). At the top of the
export revenue gainers in Sub-Saharan Africa was Côte d'Ivoire, thanks
mainly to cocoa ($250 million) and coffee ($200 million). Other countries with large gains in export revenues include Rwanda (37 percent),
Chad (28 percent), and Tanzania (17 percent). As a share of GDP, the
increase in export revenue was more than 30 percent for Ethiopia and
almost 6 percent for Côte d'Ivoire (table 4). In addition to Sub-Saharan
countries several commodity-dependent Latin American countries benefited from the boom, mainly the coffee exporters.

Table 3. Export revenues from booming commodities, by region
(billions of dollars)

Region	1992	1993	1994
East Asia and the Pacific	9.0	9.1	13.4
Europe and Central Asia	3.1	4.3	6.4
Latin America and the Caribbean	13.2	12.2	17.8
Middle East and North Africa	0.4	0.5	0.6
South Asia	1.0	0.8	0.7
Sub-Saharan Africa	5.7	5.4	7.2

Source: Estimates by the Commodity Policy and Analysis Unit, International Economics
Department, World Bank.

Table 4. Big winners, ranked by primary commodity export revenues
(billions of dollars)

Country	1992	1993	1994	Increase as % of '93 GDP
Malaysia	3.4	3.4	5.2	2.7
Brazil	2.8	2.9	4.5	0.3
Former Soviet Union	2.0	3.2	4.7	0.2
Indonesia	2.6	2.7	3.9	0.8
Colombia	1.5	1.3	2.4	1.9
Côte d'Ivoire	1.2	1.2	1.7	5.9
Thailand	1.2	1.2	1.7	0.4
Mexico	0.6	0.6	1.0	0.1
Argentina	0.6	0.7	1.1	0.2
Ethiopia	0.1	0.2	0.4	30.4

Source: Estimates by the Commodity Policy and Analysis Unit, International Economics
Department, World Bank.

Managing booms and busts

Commodity booms and busts create two types of problems: those arising from fluctuations in income and those related to the fact that fluctuations in income take the form of changes in the supply of foreign exchange. The role of policymakers is to devise ways to smooth out the impact of such income fluctuations on the economy.

The long-term effects of commodity booms are not always good. This paradox is often known as "Dutch disease." During the 1960s Dutch manufacturing suffered from the appreciation of the real exchange rate when natural gas exports boomed following discoveries in the North Sea. Commodity booms and busts can also cause other problems, such as misallocation of investment resources and financial difficulties for exporters. Exporters' financial problems occur when they sell forward at fixed prices commodities that they do not own. If prices rise sharply (above the forward sales price), exporters must make up the difference.

A buoyant export commodity in one sector often leads to declines in nonbooming export sectors. Resources flow into the booming sector, while investments elsewhere decline. Thus commodity booms tend to shift profitability among tradables as resources shift to the booming business. They can also shift profitability from tradables to nontradables since some of the incremental foreign exchange earnings from the commodity boom will be spent on nontraded goods. For this to happen, foreign exchange earnings need to be sold for local currency. If the exchange rate is floating, the currency will appreciate; if it is fixed, the money supply will rise and local prices with it and hence the currency appreciates.

Overvaluation of the currency can persist for some time after the boom ends. Past commodity booms have been followed by sharp and prolonged price declines. The overall result? The profitability of the once-booming export commodity is severely reduced, while other export subsectors have been devastated by the large real appreciation of the currency.

Commodity booms can also affect the government's budget deficit. When export commodity prices soar, government revenues usually increase sharply. This occurs directly if the resources are owned by the public sector, as is common in petroleum and mining and minerals, or indirectly, through increased export and import taxes and higher income tax revenues. The boost in revenues can encourage governments to commit to long-term and expensive programs and projects. When commodity prices decline, so do government revenues, but not expenditures. As a result, countries are often worse off than before the boom. Witness Colombia, Kenya, and Tanzania after coffee prices boomed in the late 1970s. In the post–oil boom Nigeria of the 1970s and early 1980s, the shortfall of revenues was so severe that external borrowing had risen dramatically even before oil prices began to fall. It was much the same story in Mexico's and Venezuela's handling of their oil booms. Also, since governments tend to increase their expenditures with the windfall tax revenue, fiscal policy tends to be procyclical and hence causes instability in the economy. This, according to Cuddington, has a detrimental impact on long-term economic growth (Cuddington 1988).

For many commodity-exporting countries, borrowing in global markets is not an option. For them, international loans tend to be available when they are not needed (when commodity prices are high) and unavailable when they are needed (when prices are low).

Trade policies can also partly determine the effects of a commodity boom. If they prevent revenues from being spent on imports, trade restrictions may lead to further appreciation of the exchange rate. Such restrictions may also skew income distribution. In Kenya after the 1976–79 coffee boom, import and capital controls increased rents to suppliers of capital goods and imported consumer goods so that much of the gain from the boom went to urban dwellers, who are the suppliers of the goods, and not to farmers.

In several commodity-dependent countries, particularly in Africa, significant antiexport bias already exists because of macroeconomic instability, import protection, and aid inflows. Therefore, avoiding the Dutch disease is especially important for these countries.

Learning from experience

Governments have taken various measures to stabilize revenues, neutralize the impact of foreign exchange inflows, and avoid the onset of Dutch disease. They have adopted prudent fiscal policies, liberalized import restrictions and removed capital controls, tightened monetary policies, accumulated foreign reserves, and reduced foreign debt. But what were the specific measures, and how effective were they?

Export taxes. In the latest coffee boom, Cameroon, Côte d'Ivoire, Honduras, Uganda, Viet Nam, and others reintroduced export taxes. Such taxes, so the argument goes, can alleviate both the spending and the resource movement effects of the boom and protect nonbooming tradable sectors. Tax revenues should be invested in high-yielding public investment programs that increase long-term growth.

In practice, however, tax rates are usually set too high, and public investment projects are often selected on noneconomic grounds. This tends to damage the booming sector with little compensation elsewhere in the economy. And there is the general risk of larger future deficits if the government makes long-term commitments based on boom-time tax revenues.

Excessively high export taxes can cause other problems, such as tax evasion and smuggling, that can lower tax revenues and cause serious disruptions in the domestic market for the booming commodity. Uganda imposed an export tax of 32 percent on coffee in November 1994. Some exporters did not pay the tax and, as a result, were able to pay growers higher prices. Exporters who paid the tax (but still had to match the tax-dodgers' farm-gate price) are now, apparently, in financial trouble. Low to moderate export taxes (acting as a windfall profit tax), however, could have beneficial effects by reducing overinvestment in the booming sector and providing incentives for diversification. Given the actual and potential problems, policymakers should be careful when using export taxes to manage commodity booms and busts, particularly when setting the level of the taxes.

Commodity boom bonds. In the late 1970s and the mid-1980s coffee bonds were issued by the Colombian central bank to private coffee exporters or the Federation of Coffee Growers in exchange for dollar-denominated bonds as partial payment for export sales of coffee. The coffee bonds were particularly important for altering the monetary impact of the coffee boom. The bonds acted as forced savings in foreign exchange kept at the central bank and sterilized foreign exchange inflows by reducing their impact on the monetary base. An advantage of such bonds is that they are usually more readily acceptable to the private sector than export taxes. However, boom bonds often involve some export taxation in disguise. Certainly this was true in Colombia in the late 1970s, when the government negotiated with the Coffee Growers Federation to get its members to accept bonds bearing less than the current market rate of interest—an implicit tax.

The bonds would have had different consequences if they had been issued by the government rather than the central bank. The government might have spent the revenues from the sales of the bonds, which would have negated the sterilization and national savings effects. In other words, if the government spends bond revenues, the effect is similar to that of exporters spending windfall revenues.

Diversification. Governments can promote diversification by using increased revenues to enhance extension and research services and to finance infrastructure projects. Diversification of export commodities should, in general, contribute to the alleviation of Dutch disease. Using some of the income from high coffee prices in the early and mid-1980s, the Colombian Federation of Coffee Growers launched a diversification program in coffee growing areas. The Federation undertook research on alternative crops that could be produced in coffee-growing areas and provided coffee farmers with extension services. For lower-income countries the lesson of diversification is that failing to attach a sufficiently high priority to agriculture while favoring other sectors is counterproductive. Many of these countries undertook industrialization projects to diversify their economies without giving due consideration to physical and human infrastructure. The experience of rapidly growing Asian economies indicates that a dynamic agricultural sector constitutes an important ingredient for successful diversification and, eventually, industrialization.

Hedging. Hedging increases the predictability of future revenues, reduces uncertainty, and makes planning easier. Hedging can also assist governments and the private sector to smooth short-term price fluctuations and adjust to new commodity price trends. Governments and the private sector can iron out fluctuations in future revenues by using options, swaps, and futures. The Mexican government used such hedging tools to ensure a guaranteed price for its oil (and predictable revenues) after the Gulf war. At that time, oil price uncertainty and volatility were high. One of the fears was that prices might collapse if the war ended quickly—which it did. Between December 1990 and February 1991, through the use of a complex mix of oil futures, options, and swaps, Mexico hedged about six months of oil exports. It was thus ensured of a fixed (and known) revenue, allowing policymakers time for adjustment when prices did collapse.

Governments can also use risk management tools to protect prices and stabilize the revenues of small holders, who operate at volumes that are too small to make it attractive to directly apply risk management instruments. For example, consider a country such as Mexico, which offers a guaranteed minimum price to cotton growers prior to planting. By offering the guarantee, the government has assumed on behalf of the farmer the risk that cotton prices will fall below that minimum. In many countries with minimum price guarantees, the treasury ultimately bears the cost of such programs. In Mexico, however, a government agency purchases options in the international market, transferring the risk off the government books. The cost of the option is known when the guarantee is issued and remains fixed even though the eventual cotton price is uncertain. In Mexico the cost of the program is charged back to the participating cotton farmers, with little cost to the government. The United States (for grains) and Canada (for cattle) are experimenting with futures and options to provide protection to their farmers. These instruments are usually less costly than traditional policy intervention. Government offers of risk management instruments can be particularly useful during periods of transition from government control to markets, before viable private sector risk sharing and risk management arrangements have had time to develop.

Traders and producers, too, can benefit from hedging. They stand to incur big losses if the price of a commodity rises sharply and unexpectedly after they have committed to deliver the commodity, which they do not yet own, at some fixed (and lower) price. Exporters would lose because they would have to pay much higher prices to farmers than the committed price. Similarly, traders might contract to buy the commodity from farmers at a fixed price in the future but would suffer if the price fell. They would receive a lower price when selling the commodity, and that price might not cover the higher price they paid to farmers. Indonesian coffee exporters are said to have gone bankrupt or suffered mammoth losses in the mid-1980s (and in this past year) because they did not take appropriate hedging actions. Ugandan coffee traders face similar problems.

Market-based risk management instruments are good for dealing with relatively short-lived price disruptions, because of their maturities and market liquidity. Agricultural commodities are a case in point. Maturities and liquidity for metals and energy are longer, making longer-term hedging feasible.

Hedging involves certain costs. The use of futures involves margin payments that at times could create cash-flow problems. Options involve the payment of a premium (if bought), which is the cost of insurance against price declines (put options) or increases (call options). Many countries face creditworthiness problems in accessing swaps and commodity-linked bonds. At times there is negative publicity associated with the use of hedging instruments; for example, locking in a price for exports and then witnessing a price rise. Also, hedging often requires establishing a hedging program, such as installing appropriate accounting and monitoring systems and training people to trade. These costs should be compared with the benefits from reduced uncertainty.

How much should a country or a private firm hedge? This depends on a number of factors. Among the most important are the identification of the risks of not hedging, the risk aversion of the firm (or government), the volatility in the market, and so on.

Finally, hedging that uses market-based financial instruments addresses price uncertainty, and may not necessarily stabilize revenues. However, in most cases the volatility mainly comes from prices rather than from output. In this case, these instruments assist in stabilizing revenues.

One caveat: hedging instruments need to be traded by professionals and with a clear hedging purpose. If mismanaged or used for outright speculation, they can cause as much or more damage (because of leverage) as unhedged movements in prices. Thus the use of hedging instruments by countries with poor credit ratings and weak administrative capacities is problematic.

Access to financial markets. In many countries there are few alternatives to the booming sector for investment. Liberalizing and developing financial markets can provide options for alternative investments. Underdeveloped domestic financial and capital markets may not be much of a problem, however, if producers can invest freely abroad.

Contingent borrowing facilities. Many commodity-exporting countries have little or no access to international lenders when they need it most—that is, when prices have nose-dived. Contingent borrowing facilities, such as the Compensatory and Contingency Financing Facility of the IMF and the European Union's STABEX, are designed mainly to deal with temporary shortfalls in commodity export revenues after a boom. These programs provide lending after a country is identified as having suffered substantial export revenue shortfalls.

Revenue stabilization funds. Another way to manage commodity price shocks is to create a stabilization fund—not to support or stabilize commodity prices but to provide a guide for stabilizing government expenditures. Chile has such a fund for copper (box 2). By saving resources in boom years, governments can reduce the need to cut spending in leaner times. A well-designed fund can smooth expenditure adjustments upwards or downwards. Reserves in stabilization funds should be treated as international foreign reserves.

Stabilization funds are like commodity boom bonds, sterilizing foreign exchange inflows resulting from a boom. Funds may encounter difficulties, however. Price slumps tend to last much longer than booms, so to achieve stabilization, large reserves need to be deposited into the fund, and that could imply financial costs in terms of forgone opportunities for other profitable investments. A large fund is also often not feasible for domestic political reasons, because of spending pressures from domestic constituencies. And even with large deposits, there is still the possibility that a fund may go bust. The viability of such funds depends largely on how long the commodity price change lasts and on the stabilization rule adopted. If exogenous shocks have a persistent effect on prices (or prices revert to their mean slowly), the financial soundness of the stabilization fund will ultimately come into question. Stabilization funds could also be subject to mismanagement of their resources—somewhat similar to problems encountered with export taxes. However, this is not as great a danger as in the case of tax revenues, since stabilization fund revenues are not included in general government revenues. The fund also provides clear rules on when these revenues should be spent, which is not the case with export taxes. Stabilization funds may be useful when domestic financial markets are not well developed, and there are borrowing constraints. Also, a fund may be useful when an economy bears significant costs when it adjusts spending in response to commodity booms and busts.

The workings of a stabilization fund can be complemented with market-based hedging instruments, such as futures, options, and swaps. Market-based hedging instruments are ideal for reducing the exposure to commodity price uncertainty, and a stabilization fund can reduce the instability in government revenues (or expenditures) caused by commodity price changes. Combining the stabilization fund with hedging reduces the probability that the stabilization fund will run out of reserves and allows the fund to be significantly smaller.

However, it should be noted that the international experience with stabilization funds is that most of them run into financial difficulties. Thus policymakers should be particularly cautious when deciding to adopt such a scheme.

International commodity agreements. During the late 1970s and the 1980s many commodity-producing countries attempted to stabilize commodity prices through international agreements. These included the

Box 2. Chile's copper stabilization fund

Chile's copper stabilization fund was established in 1985 as part of the government's structural adjustment program with the World Bank. The fund uses foreign exchange reserves to flatten cyclical variations in revenues. The government sets a reference price for copper (related to some moving average of international copper prices). When the actual price rises above the reference price, a portion of the excess revenue received by the government is deposited into the fund. The government can withdraw funds when the market price is below the reference price. The fund's reserves are treated as international reserves and are kept by the central bank in an offshore account. When copper prices were high in the late 1980s, accumulated reserves in the fund were used to buy back some of Chile's external debt.

International Coffee Agreement, which used an export quota system, and the International Cocoa Agreement and the International Natural Rubber Agreement, which used buffer stocks. Only the rubber agreement is still in force—just barely. Its effectiveness is being questioned by some signatories.

In January 1995 some coffee-exporting countries introduced a stock retention scheme to peg high world coffee prices. Exporters are to stockpile a percentage of exportable production (that is, production minus domestic consumption). This scheme will be difficult to maintain, however, even if all exporting countries join the program. (If only some exporters join, the free-rider problem arises with countries that benefit from the scheme but that do not participate in its costs. In the case of coffee, the costs would be administrative and storage costs.) If world prices are kept artificially high, production would likely increase. But would countries be willing to accumulate ever-increasing stocks?

Cocoa exporters, too, have recently been discussing plans to cut production—by 375,000 tons over the next five years—or to stockpile cocoa to boost (and to some extent stabilize) world prices. As with any other commodity agreement, there is the free-rider problem, which is likely to undermine the scheme. More generally, experience with price

Box 3. Colombia's tale of two booms

In the past 20 years, Colombia has seen three major coffee booms—in 1976–80, in 1986, and again in 1994. The first two booms were handled in different ways. In the 1976–80 boom, inappropriate fiscal and monetary policies meant that government expenditures began expanding rapidly in 1977 and accelerated in 1978 after prices peaked. Most of the increases were in government consumption. Meanwhile, revenues grew modestly and the fiscal deficit expanded, financed by increased foreign borrowing. With no reduction in government net credit to offset the large build up of foreign reserves, the monetary base expanded. The exchange rate appreciated in real terms by 30 percent between 1975 and 1982. Noncoffee exports declined from 7.7 percent of GDP in 1976 to 4.3 percent by 1983, completely reversing the diversification efforts in 1967–74.

In the 1986 boom, the government responded with less expansionary fiscal and monetary policies. Most of the increased revenues were held by the National Coffee Fund. Some were invested in dollar-denominated instruments, some used to purchase bonds form the central bank, and some to repay external debt. The net effect was to sterilize about 60 percent of the windfall revenues though external debt repayments and about 20 percent through open-market operations. Only 20 percent of the increased revenues entered the money supply. On the fiscal side, coffee tax revenues were used to turn a deficit of 5.2 percent of GDP in 1984 into a small surplus in 1986.

stabilization programs (buffer stocks and export quotas) suggests that market intervention is likely to fail in the long run. When that happens, commodity prices usually plunge. Witness coffee prices after July 1989, when coffee-exporting countries started to release the large stocks they had accumulated when export quotas were in force.

Fiscal discipline in response to commodity price booms. Recent research is pointing to the structure of the budgetary process as a key determinant of the nature of the response to terms of trade windfalls. One problem is the existence of multiple claimants to the increase in revenues. These could be powerful ministries, interest groups, and state-owned enterprises. Multiple claimants may appropriate more than the entire pool of revenues, diverting it to less-productive activities that benefit their constituencies. Although it is in the interest of all claimants not to squander the revenue pool, individual claimants have no incentive to act prudently if there are no guarantees that other claimants will do likewise. This line of research suggests that prudent management of commodity price booms could include changing budgetary procedures to make it less likely that fiscal windfalls will be squandered. Greater centralization of control over budget procedures might be one way to hold down the number of claimants to windfall revenues. If the proposed solution is a revenue stabilization fund, the analysis highlights the importance of strictly isolating the surpluses accumulated in the fund from the general pool of revenues. Research also shows that commodity-dependent countries often suffer from severe terms of trade shocks, and this, in turn, has had detrimental effects on their long-term economic growth and investment.

Who manages the boom?

At first glance, it seems that any boom might be more easily managed—and the impact of Dutch disease softened—if commodity prices were controlled by government (through a marketing board, for instance). The government need not raise taxes because it could administratively maintain fixed internal prices. Evidence suggests, however, that this could cause more serious problems of adjustment. Experience in Colombia and francophone Sub-Saharan Africa shows that officially set producer prices are not insensitive to world market conditions. When a world commodity price increases sharply (for coffee, for example) there is pressure to raise domestic producer prices. When the boom ends, however, governments find it difficult to lower producer prices. Indeed, governments often subsidize commodity prices after the boom to make up the difference between producer prices and export prices, leading to serious fiscal problems. That happened in Côte d'Ivoire in the late 1980s when world cocoa prices declined and in Colombia in the early 1990s when world coffee prices declined.

Some economists argue that booms and (especially) busts that are obviously temporary are far from typical. More common are the long and unforeseen commodity price slumps, like those of the late 1980s and the 1990s. Even when the booms are correctly perceived as temporary (the oil price boom in 1990–91, for instance), governments immediately spend the windfall revenues. Look at Nigeria, where the government spent quickly and, from the perspective of long-term growth, poorly.

So, if the track record of governments in managing booms is far from impressive, often because of weak administrative capacity, what about farmers? There are arguments in favor of leaving at least part of revenue stabilization to farmers. Much of the debate hinges on whether farmers can make the right choices. The evidence, while far from complete, is favorable. During boom times, some farmers have used the windfall gains in a rational manner. Kenyan coffee farmers understood the temporary nature of the coffee price boom in the late 1970s and saved about 60 percent of their extra income. Rice farmers in Thailand smooth their consumption both within and between harvest years. It is not necessarily true, therefore, that in the absence of government stabilization programs farmers would overplant in response to temporarily high prices, so long as there are alternative economic activities open to them.

The prudent behavior of farmers, however, may still be frustrated by Dutch disease or by an otherwise inappropriate macroeconomic environment (limited access to foreign exchange, for instance). Controls on imports and restrictions on investing abroad make this all the more likely. The implications for policy are that governments should allow the private sector to play a bigger part in stabilizing fluctuations in commodity-related income. That is likely to be effective, however, only if other reforms on market and financial liberalization are undertaken simultaneously.

Alternative policies for coping with the problems of commodity booms, and with price volatility more generally, generate different sets of winners. For example, export taxes instituted during boom years will permanently transfer large sums from low-income farmers and the rural sector to the government. Alternatively, if farmers hold the windfall gains as savings in foreign currency bonds, most of the benefits from the boom remain with them.

How to manage booms

Since the recent price increases are expected to be short-lived, developing countries should manage the bumper revenues carefully. Experience has shown that countries that adopted prudent fiscal and monetary policies, accumulated reserves, reduced foreign debt, and liberalized capital controls and import restrictions saw long-term beneficial results from commodity booms. Other, complementary policies have also been suggested. These policies could provide additional benefits, depending on the conditions of the economies concerned and the nature of the boom. Policies employed to manage commodity windfall revenues are:

Don't overspend or overcommit. Governments should not commit to long-term spending that will be unsustainable when the boom fizzles. The experience of the 1970s shows that countries that adopted aggressive spending programs expecting the high prices to be permanent faced huge debt-servicing problems when prices (and revenues) fell. To prevent this, a large slice of the incremental revenues should be used to build up international reserves, to be used when the boom ends.

Adopt prudent monetary and fiscal policies. Commodity-dependent countries are more vulnerable to external shocks, making sound macroeconomic policies especially critical. In this context, monetary and fiscal policies should not be expansionary, and countries could even consider reducing external debt with the proceeds from the boom. Recent research shows that commodity-dependent countries often suffer from low economic growth because of wide fluctuations in their terms of trade.

Monetary policy should balance concerns over inflation with concerns over currency appreciation. Capital-account controls (restrictions on investing abroad) and import controls should be reduced to provide a way for foreign exchange to flow out without affecting the monetary base. Investing part of the boom proceeds in foreign assets will sterilize foreign exchange inflows and avoid expansion of the monetary base. Similarly, commodity boom bonds can be viewed as savings in foreign currency and as another effective way to sterilize foreign exchange inflows.

Consider trade liberalization. Governments should consider taking advantage of the favorable trade balance situation to liberalize import restrictions. This will hold down real exchange appreciation and improve economic efficiency. If windfalls are used to finance trade liberalization, there will be permanent income gains and trade diversification, and the economy will be in much better shape after the boom than it was before.

Diversify and adjust. Governments could facilitate diversification by using incremental revenues to enhance extension and research services and finance infrastructure projects. Along with diversification, structural adjustment programs should be implemented to increase economic efficiency, particularly in the booming sectors. It is less painful to begin such programs when prices are high, and sectors will be better able to cope with lower commodity prices when the boom subsides.

A stabilization fund may be an option under some circumstances. By saving revenues in boom years, governments can iron out expenditure adjustments upward or downward and reduce the need to cut spending in leaner times. The funds should be treated as international foreign reserves. However, funds often run into financial difficulties because of the unpredictability of commodity price behavior. They are also subject to mismanagement.

Hedge. Market-based hedging instruments (futures, options, swaps) can increase the predictability of anticipated commodity-related revenues and make planning easier for policymakers. They can also assist private sector exporters and traders in handling their commodity price risks. When complementing a stabilization fund, these instruments can iron out flows into and out of the fund. Because hedging is a form of price insurance, it comes at a cost. Elements of this cost include the options premium, the opportunity cost of margin accounts, and the administrative costs for setting up and running a hedging program. These costs should be compared with the benefits of hedging—a reduction in uncertainty and a smoothing of short-term price fluctuations. Only countries with good credit ratings and appropriate administrative capacity should consider using hedging instruments.

Avoid punitive export taxes. High taxes may encourage tax evasion and smuggling. Moreover, governments tend to spend incremental tax revenues swiftly and poorly. And export taxes can only offset foreign exchange inflows if the tax proceeds are held in foreign assets. However, some level of taxation could reduce overinvestment in the booming sector and provide an incentive for diversification.

Avoid cartels—they don't work. International agreements (on buffer stocks and export quotas) are unlikely to keep commodity prices high and stable in long run. In the past, many commodity-exporting countries have entered such agreements in an attempt to stabilize and, in many cases, raise prices. In anything but the short term, none has succeeded.

References

Adams, Robin G. (Resource Strategies, Inc.). 1995. Interview in *The Financial Times*, March 31.

Bauer, Peter. 1984. "Remembrance of Studies Past: Retracing First Steps." In Gerald M. Meier and Dudley Seers, eds., *Pioneers in Development*. New York: Oxford University Press.

Claessens, S., and R. C. Duncan. 1993. *Managing Commodity Price Risk in Developing Countries*. Baltimore: The Johns Hopkins University Press for the World Bank.

Corden, W. M. 1984. "Booming Sector and Dutch Disease Economics: Survey and Consolidation." *Oxford Economic Papers* 36: 359–80.

Cuddington, J. 1988. "Fiscal Policy in Commodity-Exporting LDCs." Policy Research Working Paper 33. World Bank, Washington, D.C.

Davis, Jeffrey M. 1983. "The Economic Effects of Windfall Grains in Export Earnings, 1975–78." *World Development* 11: 119–39.

Deaton, A. "Commodity Prices, Stabilization, and Growth in Africa." Discussion Paper 166. Princeton University, Woodrow Wilson School, Research Program in Development Studies, Princeton, N.J.

Edwards, S. 1984. "Coffee, Money, and Inflation in Colombia." *World Development* 12 (11/12): 1107–17.

Gilbert, L. C. 1994. "Commodity Fund Activity and the World Cocoa Market." London Commodity Exchange.

Hill, C. B. 1991. "Managing Commodity Booms in Botswana." *World Development* 19 (9): 1185–96.

Hill, Polly. 1963. *The Migrant Cocoa Farmers of Southern Ghana: A Study in Rural Capitalism*. Cambridge: Cambridge University Press.

Killick, Tony. 1984. "Kenya, 1975–81." In Tony Killick, ed., *The IMF and Stabilization*. London: Heinemann.

Little, I. M. D., R. N. Cooper, W. M. Corden, and S. Rajapatirana. 1995. *Boom, Crisis, and Adjustment: The Macroeconomic Experience of Developing Countries*. New York: Oxford University Press for the World Bank.

Paxson, Christina H. 1992. "Using Weather Variability to Estimate the Response of Savings to Transitory Income in Thailand." *American Economic Review* 82: 15–33.

Scherr, S. J. 1989. "Agriculture in an Export Boom Economy: A Comparative Analysis of Policy and Performance in Indonesia, Mexico, and Nigeria." *World Development* 17 (4): 543–60.

Tornell, A., and P. Lane. 1994. "Are Windfalls a Curse? A Non-Representative Agent Model of the Current Account and Fiscal Policy." NBER Working Paper 4839. National Bureau of Economic Research, Cambridge, Mass.

World Bank. 1991. *World Development Report 1991: The Challenge of Development.* New York: Oxford University Press.

_____. 1994. *World Development Report 1994: Infrastructure for Development.* New York: Oxford University Press.

_____. 1995. *Commodity Markets and the Developing Countries* 2 (2). Washington, D.C.